KEEPERS OF THE VINEYARD

A People Without A Knowledge Of Their
History Is Like A Vineyard Without Fruit

DR. BARBARA SINGLETON PH.D.

WESTBOW
PRESS°
A DIVISION OF THOMAS NELSON
& ZONDERVAN

Scripture taken from the Amplified Bible, Copyright © 1954, 1958, 1962, 1964, 1965, 1987 by The Lockman Foundation. Used by permission.

Scripture taken from the King James Version of the Bible.

All inquiries should be addressed to:
Temple of Faith Apostolic Ministries, Inc.
C/O Christian Education Department
ATTN: Barbara Singleton
4908 Glenoak Drive
Killeen, Texas 76542

WestBow Press books may be ordered through booksellers or by contacting:

WestBow Press
A Division of Thomas Nelson & Zondervan
1663 Liberty Drive
Bloomington, IN 47403
www.westbowpress.com
1 (866) 928-1240

ISBN: 978-1-5127-4268-8 (sc)
ISBN: 978-1-5127-4269-5 (e)

Print information available on the last page.

WestBow Press rev. date: 05/20/2016

CONTENTS

ACKNOWLEDGMENTS

This manual is dedicated to all the ministers of the Gospel of Jesus Christ who either directly or indirectly has contributed to this work. Because of their input in my life, I was able to prosper and grow in the ministry. My desire to live for Jesus has been greatly enhanced through their leadership abilities as well as their determination to exhibit true faithfulness to God. These preachers and teachers have taught me that it is not just the negative forces, experiences, and adversities that stimulate spiritual growth, but also the positive challenges, experiences, and the victories won.

A hearty word of thanks goes out to all who have supported me through prayer and fasting. Your confidence in me has enabled me to become who I am today.

Special thanks are extended to the following saints who have labored tirelessly to help bring this manual to fruition: Evangelist Karen McClendon, Evangelist Delores Canada, Evangelist Latriece Nichols, Evangelist Kathy Kirkland, Elder Harold Hamilton, Sister Sindi Hamilton, Minister Floyd Chambers, Sister Virginia Parker, and Sister Latese Jamison. God Speed!

Last but not least, a heartfelt- thank you goes out to my companion, Willie Singleton Sr.; my daughter, LaTasha Thompson; my grandson, Yemauri Thompson, and my granddaughter, Aaliyah Simmons for their love and support.

"God is not unrighteous to forget your work and labor of love, which you have showed toward His name, in that you have ministered to the saints, and do minister" (Hebrew 6:10).

PREFACE

This study guide is intended to be a guide for individuals who desire to learn more about missionary work. It does not aim to cover every subject concerning the missionary and his mission, but rather to set forth in an abridged form a working knowledge of the missionary and his duty to win souls for the Lord.

Jesus commanded his disciples to go into all the world to preach the gospel to every creature (Mark 16:15). A missionary is one of the tools that God uses to evangelize the world. God realizes that, in addition to knowledge, other qualities are necessary for a missionary to become successful on the missionary field. Some of these qualities are less tangible but must exist concurrently for an individual to achieve that success.

Missionaries are reflections of Jesus Christ; when others see them, they see what they ought to be. God has set missionaries in the church for the purpose of picking up the pieces of weak and shattered lives and putting them back together again (Acts 13:47).

In *The New American Webster Dictionary*, a missionary is defined as "one sent to spread religion or philosophy in a foreign land or to persons not of the same persuasion."

In this study guide, I will introduce you to the life of a missionary as it relates to his purpose, place, position, and work in the church and community. It is my desire that this manual will be a blessing to all.

CHAPTER 1

The Qualifications of a Missionary

*W*ebster's Collegiate Dictionary defines qualification as a "quality or skill that fits a person for an office; a condition or standard that must be complied with for the attainment of a privilege." Qualification is the skill, knowledge, and experience, that fits a person for a position, office, or profession.

THIS IS A TRUE SAYING: IF YOU DESIRE THE OFFICE OF A MISSIONARY, YOU DESIRE A GOOD WORK.

ATTRIBUTES

There are some basic attributes that contribute to the success of an effective missionary ministry. Here is a listing of some of them:

- A person must be blameless, the person of one spouse, vigilant, sober, of good behavior, given to hospitality, apt to teach
- Not given to wine, no striker, not greedy of filthy lucre; but patient, not a brawler, not covetous
- Must have a good report among those which are outside
- Must preserve the truth in a pure conscience
- Must rule his children and household well

- Live a quiet and peaceable life in all godliness and honesty
- Must adorn self in modest apparel, with shamefacedness and sobriety
- Be of an honest report, full of the Holy Ghost and wisdom

The following scriptures can be used to support this:

1 Timothy 3:1-3, 7, 9, 12
1 Timothy 2:9

The following characteristics must also be present: "Love, joy, peace, longsuffering, gentleness, goodness, faith, meekness, and temperance: against such there is no law" (Galatians 5:22-23).

Note: The subject matter stated above comes from the scriptures based on the office of a bishop or deacon, but the same principles are applied to the office of a missionary.

CHAPTER 2

Leadership Versus Lordship

The Webster's Collegiate Dictionary lists among the definitions of the words *lead* and *lord* the following: To lead is "to guide on a way, especially by going in advance; to serve as a channel for; to direct the operations, activities, or performance of; to have charge of." Lord is defined as "to exercise dominion and authority over." Its Biblical usage connotes "to rule with force and cruelty; to be harsh" (Matthew 20:25-28; Ezekiel 34:4).

First Peter 5:1-4 of the *Amplified Bible* reads, "I warn and counsel the elders among you (the pastors and spiritual guides of the church) . . . Tend (nurture, guard, guide, and fold) the flock of God . . . not by coercion or constraint, but willingly; . . . Not domineering [as arrogant, dictatorial, and overbearing persons] over those in your charge, but being examples (patterns and models of Christian living) to the flock (the congregation). And (then) when the Chief Shepherd is revealed, you will win the conqueror's crown of glory."

Those desiring to become effective leaders should apply these charges to themselves. A leader is a role model for others to observe and see what they ought to be.

3

KEY POINTS TO REMEMBER

- Focus on nurturing, guarding, guiding, and embracing those in your care.
- Serve not by constraint, but willingly.
- Strive not for dishonest gain.
- Be an example of good works.
- A crown of glory awaits you.

THINGS TO CONSIDER WHEN SELECTING LEADERS

- Honesty, reputation, outside report 1 Timothy 3:7
- Full of Holy Ghost and wisdom Acts 6:3
- Ability to acknowledge others' worth Romans 13:7
- Compassionate spirit Galatians 5:22-23
- An effective listener James 1:19
- A good follower makes a good leader John 5:19

AN EFFECTIVE LEADER . . .

- Is an industrious person
- Carries the bulk of the load
- Takes his position seriously
- Never waits until the last minute to plan
- Must stay focused
- Takes up the slack of his peers
- Is able to take charge, settle disputes, and combat strife
- Leads by example in attitude, behavior, self-esteem, promptness, obedience, etc.
- Is informative
- Knows his peers by name, performance, and spirit
- Strives toward excellence
- Must be able to use his time wisely
- Puts others first

- Is able to cope or adjust to sudden changes
- Gives respect to receive respect from others
- Is responsible for the actions of his peers
- Is a servant above the rest

CHAPTER 3

Functions of the Home Missionary

The home missionary call has many functions depending on the needs of the church. According to *The New American Webster Dictionary*, a missionary is defined as "one sent to spread religion or philosophy in a foreign land or to persons not of the same persuasion."

A missionary, under the leadership of God, has the ability to encourage, to strengthen, and to confirm the will of God to others. The missionary holds a high position in today's church. As in all other positions, he is a servant of the people, not vice versa. He must be compassionate and patient with others and learn how to rule his own spirit.

Most missionaries today have a demanding job in their home churches. Several duties of the home missionary may include:

- Training individuals on how to respond to various situations relating to winning souls
- Consoling those who have been wounded by the Word of God
- Assisting in deliverance services
- Encouraging backsliders to return to God

- Taking an interest in the young adults through seminars, programs, etc.
- Helping to establish baby saints in the church

Junior missionaries can be of assistance by:

- Greeting visiting children before and after church services
- Assisting children to their seats after the altar call
- Furnishing paper towels and altar sheets as needed
- Sitting with children while they wait for after-baptism counseling

The home missionary often offers his or her services in hospital rooms, nursing homes, foster homes, prisons, or wherever there is a soul in need. His or her goal is to spread the love of Jesus Christ to everyone by following in his footsteps.

CHAPTER 4

Preparation for Victory in Battle
Nehemiah 4:14-23, James 4:7-10

E ach individual must prepare himself for fighting Satan because we need power that we do not have within ourselves. Satan's desire is to destroy man any way that he can. Each born again believer has the power to put Satan to flight, but he needs to be fortified in order to fight. We need to be built up and encouraged. Every man will become discouraged at times. We need God's help to put Satan to flight (Deut. 32:30).

A TIME TO KILL

Eccl 3:1 says, "To everything there is a season, and a time to every purpose under heaven." The following are a few reasons to stand against the enemy of our soul:

- Tired of devil influence in your life (mind, home, finances, job, health)
- Flesh is in control: envy, jealousy, disobedience
- Blessings or promotions are cut off
- The enemy is on your trail

THE WEAPONS OF OUR WARFARE

Second Corinthians 10:4-5 declares, "For the weapons of our warfare are not carnal, but mighty through God to the pulling down of strongholds; casting down imaginations, and every high thing that exalts itself against the knowledge of God . . ." The spiritual weapons of warfare will be discussed in more detail in chapter six, but a few *must have* weapons are listed here:

- Fasting
- Prayer
- The Word of God

An effective witness for Christ must have control of his or her own spirit. Paul said, "I keep under my body, and bring it into subjection: lest . . . when I have preached to others, I myself should be a cast away" (1 Corinthians 9:27). Some things that will help in achieving the goal are to:

- Guard your own spirit (temper, tongue).
- Watch your reactions to sudden situations.
- Stop and think before you act.
- Submit your will to God.
- Rid yourself of pride.

Proverbs 4:23 declares, "Keep your heart with all diligence; for out of it are the issues of life." Here is a checklist that applies to everyone with the desire to be in right standing with God:

- Come clean, check your heart.
- Put away strife.
- Be broken and ashamed of sins.
- Lay aside weights and habitual sins.
- Pray without ceasing.

Each failure will repeat itself until the test is passed. God has given his people the authority to "[tread] on serpents and scorpion, and all the power of the enemy" (Luke 10:19).

UNANSWERED PRAYERS

There are many reasons why individual prayers go unanswered. Here is a summary of some of them:

* Unconfessed sin in the heart   Psalm 66:18
* Uncrucified Flesh   1 Corinthians 9:27
* Strife and dissension   1 Peter 3:7
* Do not believe in God   Hebrews 11:6

Paul reminded us that there is no good thing in the flesh (Romans 7:18). God is not pleased when men participate in these things: Wrath, hatred, blasphemy, cursing, lying, uncontrolled anger, and pride (Colossians 3:8).

In times like these, what a blessing it is to know that, though we live in this world, our tools of war are not carnal but spiritual. God's mighty weapons are powerful enough to pull down strongholds, cast down imaginations, and every high thing that [exalts] itself against the knowledge of God (2 Corinthians 10:4-5).

"THOU WILT KEEP HIM IN PERFECT PEACE; WHOSE MIND IS STAYED ON THEE: BECAUSE HE [TRUST] IN THEE" (ISAIAH 26:3).

It has been said that the mind is a terrible thing to lose. Satan's desire is to kill, steal, and destroy every man's relationship with God. This he does by attacking the mind. It is God's will that man would have peace.

Peace is a state of tranquility or quiet; a freedom from disquieting or oppressive thoughts or emotions. In the world, mankind is faced with so many disturbing circumstances that, more often than not, lead to confusion of the mind. God is not the author of confusion, but of peace (1 Corinthians 14:33). In the world we will have tribulation, but in Christ we can have peace (John 16:33).

CHAPTER 5

Presumptuous Sins and Secret Faults
Psalm 19:12-14; Psalm 51 chapter

P resumptuous sins and secret faults are those sins that we hide from the sight of men. They are the sins that are tucked away in our hearts. We call these sins our "dark side." Our sins are ever before us, and they try to take dominion over our will. Isaiah 59:2 and 59:12 says that, our sin separates us from God and causes him to hide his face from us. When we do not confess and forsake sins, they will multiply and testify against us.

Jesus said, "If I had not come and spoken unto them, they had not had sin: but now they have no cloak for their sin (John 15:22)." Romans 1:18-20 declares, "For the wrath of God is revealed from heaven against all ungodliness and unrighteousness of men, who hold the truth in unrighteousness; because that which may be known of God is manifest in them . . . For the invisible things of him from the creation of the world are clearly seen, being understood by the things that are made, even his eternal power and Godhead; so that they are without excuse."

SINS OF DECEPTION

Peter characterized false prophets as presumptuous because they were self-willed, despised governments and were not afraid to speak evil of dignities (2 Peter 2:10). In rebuking the Laodicean church, Jesus said, "Because thou sayest, I am rich, and increased with goods, and have need of nothing; and knowest not that thou art wretched, and miserable, and poor, and blind and naked: (Revelation 3:17)." Presumptuous sins give the impression that everything is all right on the outside while at the same time the foundation is being destroyed.

AN IMITATION WON'T DO

David pleaded, "Cleanse . . . me from secret faults . . . [and] presumptuous sins; let them not have dominion over me . . . Let the words of my mouth and the meditation of my heart be acceptable in thy sight . . ." (Psalms 19:12-14). He knew that when these sins reach your heart, they would destroy your steadfastness in the Lord. They will cause us to do what we don't want to do. Paul said, "I delight in the law of God after the inward man: but I see another law in my members, warring against the law of my mind, and bringing me into captivity to the law of sin which is in my members" (Romans 7:22-23).

Saul said, "I have sinned: yet honor me now . . ." (1 Samuel 15:30). In other words, don't chastise me; just let me continue to be a hypocrite. If you don't reveal my sins, I'll go to the temple and worship as usual.

It is not sacrifices and offerings that God desires; he wants real people to testify to his word. God is looking for someone that will cease from evil and learn to do well (Isaiah 1:16-17). Someone that will go to the altar with a bowed down head and confess, "It's me, O Lord, standing in the need of prayer. I acknowledge my transgressions and my sin is ever before me. Against thee only have I sinned, and done this evil in thy sight. I offer to you Lord, a broken and contrite spirit that you will not despise" (Psalms 51:3, 17).

CONFESSION IS GOOD FOR THE SOUL

When we have strayed and afterward realize that we want to return to God, it is to our advantage to go back to the potter's house, place ourselves upon the wheel, and ask God to restore us back again (Jeremiah 18:1-6). David cried, "Have mercy on me, O God, according to thy loving kindness . . . Wash me thoroughly from my iniquity, and cleanse me from my sin . . . Create in me a clean heart . . . and renew a right spirit within me. Restore unto me the joy of thy salvation . . ." (Psalm 51:1, 2, 10, 12).

WASH ME

"Wash me thoroughly from my iniquity, and cleanse me from my sin," said David (Psalm 51:2). "Peter said unto him, Thou shalt never wash my feet." Jesus answered him, "If I wash thee not, thou hast no part with me." "Simon Peter saith unto him, Lord, not my feet only, but also my hands and my head" (John 13:8-9). We may also want to pray, "Wash my mind so I can think right; wash my heart so I can love right; wash my attitude so I can live right. Wash me, Jesus, from the inside out."

PURGE ME

David continues, "Purge me . . . and I shall be clean" (Psalm 51:7). Every now and then we sing a song that says, "Search me Lord, let your light shine from heaven on my soul, and if you find anything that shouldn't be, take it out and strengthen me. I want to be right. I want to be saved. I want to be whole." The only way we can present our bodies as living sacrifices unto God is to allow our minds to be purged and renewed so that old things will be passed away, and we'll become new creatures in him.

A CLEAN HEART

"Create in me a clean heart . . . and renew a right spirit within me" (Psalm 51:10). When Jesus returns to take His people home (John 14:3), it will not be sacrifices and offerings that he will take notice of, but the pure hearts of those who have washed their robes in the blood of the Lamb.

JOY BELLS ARE RINGING

David said, "Restore unto me the joy of thy salvation . . ." (Psalm 51:12). When we are tangled up in sin, our joy is taken away. If I may use my Holy Ghost imagination here, this is how I would tell the story: David was sitting in the temple and the choir was singing—"Joy bells are ringing in my soul." The saints around him were singing and dancing before the Lord. The drummer, pianist, and guitar player were all praising God in music, but David could not feel the move of God's spirit. He couldn't feel the joy bells ringing, so he struck up his own tune. And it went something like this, "Something's wrong with me, Lord, something's wrong with me." About that time, he looked over at the priest, and the priest was shouting and praising God. David sang on, "There is nothing wrong with the priests, but something is wrong with me. For all I do Lord, I can't feel your spirit; there is something wrong with me." And then he said, "Restore me; take me back; give me back my joy, my peace, and my anointing."

No matter how hard we try, we cannot live holy without the Holy Ghost. We need the Holy Ghost's power to enable us to enter into the kingdom of God (John 3:3-5). Righteousness, joy, and peace are products of the Holy Ghost (Romans 14:17). The Holy Ghost is Jesus's spirit that comes to dwell inside a "born again" believer. Paul admonished us to "lay aside every weight, and the sin that doth so easily beset us, and . . . run this race with patience . . ." (Hebrews 12:1-2). Paul knew that only the pure in heart shall see God (Matthew 5:8). It is very obvious that, without Jesus we can do nothing, but with Him we can do all things (John 15:5; Philippians 4:13).

CHAPTER 6

Rendering the Devil Helpless

P aul, in his letter to the Corinthian church, says, "For though we walk in the flesh, we do not war after the flesh: For the weapons of our warfare are not carnal, but mighty through God to the pulling down of strongholds; casting down imaginations and every high thing that [exalts] itself against the knowledge of God, and bringing into captivity every thought to the obedience of Christ; And having in a readiness to revenge all disobedience, when your obedience is fulfilled" (2 Corinthians 10:3-6).

It is imperative that we understand that Satan is a spirit and cannot be fought with the tools of man. We need spiritual tools to fight spiritual battles, and even then, the battle is won only when our obedience to God's plan is fulfilled.

Strongholds are thoughts that are placed in our mind by Satan in order to produce fear in our lives with the intent of destroying us. Our thoughts become strongholds, strongholds become imaginations, and imaginations develop into fear, which will eventually destroy us.

SPIRITUAL TOOLS

There are many spiritual tools used by the people of God to fight the devil, but I will discuss only a few in this section of the book, and they are faith in God, prayer and fasting, the Word, and the power of praise.

FAITH

The Holy Bible declares, "Faith is the substance of things hoped for, the evidence of things not seen . . ." and "without faith it is impossible to please him: for he that comes to God (whether by prayer, fasting, petitions, etc.), must believe that he is God and that he is a rewarder of them that diligently seek him" (Hebrews 11:1, 6).

PRAYER AND FASTING

One day, a certain man brought his son, who was a lunatic, to the disciples for healing, but the disciples could not heal the boy. "Then came the disciples to Jesus apart, and said, 'Why could not we cast him out?' Jesus answered, 'Because of your unbelief . . . If you have faith as a grain of mustard seed you shall say unto this mountain, Remove hence to yonder place; and it shall remove; and nothing shall be impossible unto you. Howbeit this kind goes not out but by prayer and fasting" (Matthew 17:15-21). Prayer and fasting together will give us the power, through God, to work miracles.

THE WORD

The Word of God is quick, and powerful, and sharper than any two-edged sword piercing even to the dividing asunder of soul and spirit, and of the joints and marrow, and is a discerner of the thoughts and intents of the heart" (Hebrews 4:12). God's word is so powerful that when it is spoken, God's anointing backs it up and causes the demons to fear and tremble.

Saint Matthew records that, "When the tempter came to Jesus, he said, If thou be the Son of God, command that these stones be made bread. But Jesus said, It is written, Man shall not live by bread alone, but by every word that [proceed] out of the mouth of God"

(Matthew 4:4, 7). The example that Jesus left for us to whip the devil was, "It is written."

PRAISE

Praise is the magnet that pulls the blessings of God down to man. God inhabits the praises of his people (Psalms 22:3). As Paul and Silas prayed at midnight and sang praises unto God, a great earthquake formed, "so that the foundation of the prison was shaken: and immediately all the doors were opened, and every one's bands were loosed" (Acts 16:25-26).

Many battles have been won through praise. Praise equips the believer for battle by arming him with courage and strength. It sends a message to Satan that the banner of faith has been lifted and the battle has already been won.

DEMONIC ATTACKS

From day to day, the saints of God wrestle against principalities and powers of darkness. In order to stand against the wiles of the devil, one must depend on God's strength and the right armor. Jesus called Satan, the thief that comes to kill, steal, and destroy. Satan's goal is to destroy the soul, the family, and the church. However, James gave the key to overcoming demonic attacks, "Submit yourselves therefore to God. Resist the devil, and he will flee from you" (James 4:7).

KNOW YOUR ENEMY

Listed are a group of words that, when left unchecked, will produce bad fruit. The more we know about the enemy, the better we will be.

- REBELLION- God compares rebellion to the sin of witchcraft (1 Samuel 15:23).

- Rebellion leads to a self-willed spirit, stubbornness, disobedience, and a non-submissive spirit (Jonah 1:1-3; 1 Samuel 15:3, 9, 22-23).

- PRIDE – "Goes before destruction, and a haughty spirit before a fall" (Proverbs 16:18).

- Characteristics of pride are ego, vanity, self- righteousness, haughtiness, importance, and arrogance (Esther 3:1-6, 5, 9-14).

- STRIFE – "The beginning of strife is as when one let out water. Therefore leave off contention, before it be meddled with" (Proverbs 17:14). Strife leads to contention, bickering, arguments, quarreling, and fighting.

- JEALOUSY – "Is as cruel as the grave" (Song of Solomon 8:6). Jealousy brings with it envy, suspicion, distrust, and selfishness.

- INSECURITY – Leads to inferiority, self-pity, loneliness, timidity, shyness, inadequacy.

- The Lord "will keep him in perfect peace whose mind is stayed on [him]: because he [trusts in the Lord]" (Isaiah 26:3).

- CONFUSION – "In thee, O Lord, do I put my trust: let me never be put to confusion" (Psalm 71:1). The offspring of confusion are frustration, incoherence, and forget-fullness.

CHAPTER 7

Altar and Upper Room Evangelism

T he altar and the upper room are places where souls come to be birthed or to be delivered from afflictions. Altars were used in many religions, but for the people of God, they were more than just places of sacrifice. The altar symbolizes a place of communion with God, a place of worship, and a place to seek forgiveness of sins. The altar is a sacred place and plays an important role in the church of today. Service after service, the altar is lined with people that come seeking God's help.

THE ALTAR WORKER

Proverbs says, "The fruit of the righteous is a tree of life; and he that [wins] souls is wise" (Proverbs 11:30). Wisdom is knowledge. It is the ability to discern inner qualities and relationships, insight, good sense, and good judgment. Working the altar is a God-given ministry to the church. It is a gift that not everyone has. Some necessities of an altar worker are an ear to hear the voice of God, a holy lifestyle, consistency in fasting and prayer, and a spirit of discernment.

James says, "If any of you lack wisdom, let him ask of God, that [gives] to all men liberally, and upbraideth not; and it shall be given him" (James 1:5). The purpose of the altar and upper room team is to win souls for the Lord and to help souls to be delivered. The following information is only a guideline. Further instructions will come directly from God.

The hearts of souls that come to the altar have already been pricked by the Word of God. God's word is a mirror that shows a man himself. Altar workers are to be watchful and, at times, may need to go and help those individuals who are shy about coming to the altar.

AT THE ALTAR

Approach the individual and ask, "What is it that you need from the Lord?" etc. Then proceed to pray for the need. Depending on the situation or the comment, "I want to get right with God, or I want to be saved," etc., proceed to ask the questions concerning water baptism in the name of Jesus.

EXAMPLE
Ask: *Have you been baptized?*
Response: *Yes*

Ask: *How were you baptized?* Response: *In water*

Ask: *What did the preacher say?*
Response: *I don't remember* or *I'm not sure*

The correct way to be baptized is in the name of Jesus Christ. Father, Son, Holy Ghost are just titles. If you are not sure of how you were baptized, then it is better to be baptized again. I believe that you want to be right with God. Upon consent for baptism, the baptism committee takes charge.

Here is another example for when a saint needs to be delivered: Ask the question, "What do you need from the Lord?" or "What do you want me to pray for?" etc. The next step is deliverance.

21

Following are phrases that are helpful when helping saints get a breakthrough:

*Talk to Jesus	*Take Jesus at his word
*Just surrender	*Turn it over to Jesus
*Tell him all about it	*Just trust him

WHAT TO DO WHEN AN INDIVIDUAL IS TAKEN FROM THE ALTAR TO THE UPPER ROOM:

A saved person – When the person is already in the Spirit, let God have His way. There is nothing else to do but pray. If God leads you to tell them something, obey. If not, stay with the individual and be prayerful. Return to the sanctuary together.

An unsaved person – When the person is already in the Spirit, encourage him to elevate his mind so God can come in. Sometimes a person is so overwhelmed with the Spirit as he or she comes to the altar, and you don't have time to explain to them about receiving the Holy Ghost. Never break the move of the Spirit to follow a set pattern of operation. One must learn to move with the Spirit.

Phrases to use to help an individual receive the Holy Ghost are as follows:

- The Holy Ghost is a gift from God.
- Keep your mind on Jesus.
- That's the way to praise him.
- Let him in.
- Talk to Jesus in your mind.
- Let your soul say "yes."
- Yield to his will.
- Reach out to him.
- Don't stop praising him.
- Hold on to Jesus.

When the unsaved person is calm and not caught up in the Spirit, in the upper room, do the following:

- Introduce yourself and other helpers by first name.
- Explain the process for receiving the Holy Ghost.
- Give the person an opportunity for prayer and repentance.
- Inform the person that prayer will be said aloud and, at the end of the prayer, tarrying will begin
- The person may stand, kneel, or sit in a chair
- The altar worker will choose whether the seeker will tarry by saying Jesus, Hallelujah, etc. If there is more than one seeker, all will begin to say the same thing.

The altar worker is the first person to begin seeking as an example to the seeker. The difference is that the altar worker's eyes are open, and the seeker's eyes are closed.

- Use phrases from above.
- Be prayerful and watch for the enemy at all times.
- Have supplies available: paper towels, altar sheet, etc.
- Never leave the seeker alone.
- No hollering or loud hand clapping in the seeker's ear.

TESTING FOR THE HOLY GHOST

If you believe that the seeker has received the Holy Ghost and he is speaking in another language, have him say either Jesus or Hallelujah. If the seeker can continue to say Jesus or Hallelujah, then the Holy Ghost has not come. When the Holy Ghost comes, he will be in control and not the individual.

In closing:

Never tell the seeker that he has received the Holy Ghost. Let him tell you instead. However, be sure that you and a witness have both heard the tongues.

Questions you may ask when seeking is finished:

- How do you feel?
- What happened while you were praising God?
- Can you explain how you are feeling right now?
- You started out saying Jesus/Hallelujah; were you able to continue to say Jesus/Hallelujah the whole time?

It is not a bad idea to ask the saved person to come back to tarry one more time. Sometimes it makes the difference between knowing if they have the real thing or if they were only repeating what they heard someone else say.

Response – *I thank God for baptizing you with the Holy Ghost tonight. You can receive the Holy Ghost only one time, but you can be refilled many times. Would you be willing to come back tomorrow night (or next service night) for more strength? The same Jesus that spoke tonight will speak again tomorrow night. Okay, I'll see you then, if it is the Lord's will.*

If the seeker did not come through – *Jesus really blessed you tonight, but I want you to come back for more. We will continue on until the Holy Ghost comes. Be encouraged and don't give up. I'll be praying for you.*

Remember that God inhabits the praises of his people (Psalms 22:3). Praise will bring his presence near. The altar worker must become very sensitive to the Holy Ghost. When God begins to move on a person, he may initially become frightened. Talk to him and reassure him of God's presence; the candidate will then relax and allow God to take over the praise. Shortly, he will speak in another language as God gives the utterance. Allow him to speak through to deliverance.

LAYING ON OF HANDS

The laying on of hands was a Hebrew custom that was not started by divine authority, but was authorized later both in Israel (Exodus 29:10-15; Deuteronomy 34:9) and in the church (Acts 8:14-22; 19:1-7). It has been practiced publicly by man in all ages when blessing them or ordaining and separating them for a particular work for God.

The right hand of God is a symbol of power and strength (Exodus 15:6; Psalms 17:7). Laying on of hands to do God's will is an outward form of rendering a blessing unto another. Whether it is performed to receive a blessing, a healing, salvation, or deliverance, we must remember we are only vessels being used by God.

ORDAINED FOR SERVICE

And the Lord spoke unto Moses saying, "And thou shall bring the Levites before the Lord: and the children of Israel shall put their hands upon the Levites: And Aaron shall offer the Levites before the Lord for an offering of the children of Israel, that they may execute the service of the Lord" (Numbers 8:10-11).

> "Then the twelve called the multitude of the disciples unto them, and said, It is not reason that we should leave the word of God, and serve tables. Wherefore, brethren, look you out among you seven men of good report, full of the Holy Ghost and wisdom, whom we may appoint over this business . . . and when they had prayed, they laid their hands on them. And the word of God increased" (Acts 6:2-7).

TO RECEIVE SALVATION

"Now when the apostles . . . at Jerusalem heard that Samaria had received the word of God, they sent unto them Peter and John: Who, when they were come down, prayed for them that they might receive the Holy Ghost" (Acts 8:14, 15, 17).

CHAPTER 8

How to Restore a Fallen Soul

R estore, as it is defined in *Webster's Collegiate Dictionary*, means "to renew, rebuild; to put or bring back into existence or use, to bring back to or put back into a former or original state." The Amplified Bible reads, "Brethren, if any person is overtaken in misconduct or sin of any sort, you who are spiritual (who are responsive to and controlled by the spirit) should set him right and restore and reinstate him, without any sense of superiority and with all gentleness" (Galatians 6:1).

A GIFT FROM GOD

The ability to restore a person is a gift placed in the church by God. It is the work of the Holy Ghost working through us. We should pray, fast, and do all we can to excel in this gift. To love one another is a voluntary emotion that tests our love for the backslider. Second Corinthians admonishes us, as workers together with Christ, to be careful that we receive not the grace of God in vain. That we give no offense in anything, "that the ministry be not blamed: But in all things approving ourselves as the ministers of God, in much patience, in afflictions, necessities and in distresses . . . by pureness, by knowledge, by long-suffering, by kindness, by the Holy Ghost, and by love without hypocrisy" (2 Corinthians 6:1-6). The Bible is the measuring stick that we use to keep an attentive eye on ourselves, lest we be tempted to sin. Matthew tell us to treat others the way in which we wish to be treated (Matthew 7:12). The way of restoration is in the spirit of meekness.

To everything there is a season, and a time to every purpose under the heaven . . . A time to kill, and a time to heal; a time to break down, and a time to build up . . . a time to rend, and a time to sew; a time to keep silence, and a time to speak (Ecclesiastes 3:1, 3, 7). Pray for the right time to minister. It is not the will of God that "[anyone] should perish but that all should come to repentance" (2 Peter 3:9). In the spirit of restoration, "If your brother shall trespass against [you], go and tell him his fault between [you] and him alone: if he will hear [you], then [you will have] gained [your] brother. But if he will not hear [you], then take with [you] one or two more people, that in the mouth of two or three witnesses every word may be established (Matthew 18:15-16).

AT THE ALTAR

In some churches, at the end of the altar call, the "repeating offender" is asked to stand and ask the church for forgiveness. The offender would then repent and forsake his or her sins. Some backsliders need to confess before the pastor alone before coming before the congregation. "If we say that we have no sin, we deceive ourselves, and the truth is not in us. If we confess our sins, [God] is faithful and just to forgive us our sins, and to cleanse us from all unrighteousness" (1 John 1:8-9). Altar confession is done at the discretion of the pastor.

THE BACKSLIDER AND THE MISSIONARY

The missionary should be motivated and ruled by the Holy Ghost. He is to work with the candidate until he is delivered from the bondage of sin, witnessed by the evidence of speaking in other tongues. Lastly, but not least, stay in contact and encourage him to be faithful in coming to church.

CHAPTER 9

Baptism—The True Foundation

EXCEPT A MAN BE BORN OF THE WATER

"Then Peter said . . ., 'Repent, and be baptized every one of you in the name of Jesus Christ for the remission of sins, and [you] shall receive the gift of the Holy Ghost'" (Acts 2:38). Jesus answered, "Verily, verily, I say unto thee, Except a man be born of water and of the Spirit, he cannot enter into the kingdom of God" John 3:5.

Many people come to Jesus in the same fashion as that of the rich, young ruler who came to inquire what he might do to inherit eternal life. But when the truth was told, he went away in sorrow, proving that his love for the world was greater than his love for God (Mark 10:17-22).

Peter, before Annas, the high priest, stated that there is salvation in no other: "for there is none other name under heaven given among men, whereby we must be saved" (Acts 4:12). It is also stated in the scriptures, "He that [believe] and is baptized shall be saved; but he that [believe] not shall be damned" (Mark 16:16).

The only true church is the one Jesus started through his disciples in the upper room on the day of Pentecost (Acts 2:1-4). Peter preached that this miraculous event was the fulfillment of that which Joel had prophesied (Joel 2:28-32).

God's true church is symbolized as a virgin bride in the New Testament. John saw the holy city, New Jerusalem, as it came out of heaven "prepared as a bride adorned for her husband" (Revelation 21:2). Jesus Christ started the only true church. Every church that sprang up afterward is called a false church and is symbolized as a harlot church (Revelation 17:5). A harlot is a woman who enjoys all the rights of a marriage but does not have a husband. In order for a harlot to become a bride of Christ, she must take on the name of the groom (Jesus) through water baptism. To "put on Christ" is to be baptized by immersion in water in the name of Jesus Christ (Galatians 3:27). Jesus wants his people to be set apart from this sinful worldly system. God said through John the Revelator, "Come out of her, my people, that you be not partakers of her sins, and that you receive not of her plagues" (Revelation 18:4).

THE UNITY OF THE SPIRIT

Many people believe that the form of baptism stating in the name of the Father, and of the Son, and of the Holy Ghost to be the correct way to baptize, yet the Bible clearly states that there is only one Lord, one faith, and one baptism. "One God and Father of all, who is above all, through all, and in you all" (Ephesians 4:5-6), and in Him [dwells] all the fullness of the Godhead [in a bodily form]. [We] are complete in him, which is the head of all principality and power (Colossians 2:9-10).

Jesus commissioned his disciples to go into "the world and preach the gospel to every creature. He that believes and is baptized," said Jesus, "shall be saved; but he that believes not shall be damned" (Mark 16:15-16).

Matthew 28:19 says, "Go . . . and teach all nations, baptizing them in the name of the Father, and of the Son, and of the Holy Ghost." Was Peter being rebellious when he told the people to repent and be baptized in the name of Jesus Christ to wash away their sins?

No! Peter knew that these (Father, Son, Holy Ghost) were just titles. Salvation is in the name of Jesus Christ (Acts 4:12).

WHY BE BORN AGAIN

The Lord God formed man of the dust of the ground, and breathed into his nostrils the breath of life and man became a living soul (Genesis 2:7). Man consists of body, soul, and spirit. Our spirit will never die. It contains all of our senses, in this life and in the next. God made Adam perfect and without sin, but Adam fell from perfection, and his seed passed on to all generations. Since then, we all have sinned and come short of the glory of God, and we must all be born again in-order to meet Jesus in righteousness (Romans 3:23; 1 John 1:8-9; John 3:5). Cornelius was a good man, but he was lost. He needed to be born again of the water and of the Spirit (Acts 10:1-3; 11:14).

GUIDELINES FOR BAPTISM

The purpose of guidelines are to establish standards that will, by faith, be pleasing in the sight of God. The baptismal committee should consist of workers who perform duties described in these guidelines under the direction of the pastor and the missionary president.

In the baptismal area, the missionary will:

- Introduce himself by his first name only
- Read and expound on Acts 2:38 and Romans 6:1-4
- Explain to the candidate that water baptism, in Jesus' name, is for the washing away or the remission of sins (Acts 2:38) and should take place only after repentance
- Explain that baptism says goodbye to the world and embraces a new life in Christ
- Prepare the candidate for baptism with a towel, gown, slippers, and a cap

- Concentrate on the seriousness of what is about to take place, stop all idle talking
- Escort the candidate to the pool and then back to the dressing room
- Obtain contact information
- Escort the candidate to the counseling area. Never leave the candidate unattended.
- Encourage the candidate to be faithful to church services

THE OPERATION OF BAPTISM

Everyone that receives the water baptism in Jesus's name needs to understand more fully what has taken place. Baptism is more than just getting wet. The baptismal counselor should take time to explain the operation that takes place at baptism. Many things take place as a person is emerged, in that watery grave, and goes on to receive the Holy Ghost.

The following list contains a few:

- Begin the first day of one's spiritual life   Exodus 12:1-2
- Removes sins   Acts 2:38; 22:16
- Name is written in heaven   Rev. 20:12,15
- Rise to walk in the newness of life   Romans 6:4
- Become a new creature in Christ   2 Corinthians 5:17
- Take on the righteousness of God   2 Corinthians 5:21
- Places one in the church   Acts 2:47
- Transforms from the kingdom of Satan (darkness) into the kingdom of God (light)

Several supporting scriptures for Matthew 28:19 are Mark 16:16, Luke 24:47, and Acts 10:48

Scripture of proof: 2 Corinthians 13:1, "In the mouth of two or three witnesses shall every word be established."

IN SEARCH FOR THE TRUE CHURCH

In our society, there are two basic groups of people: those who baptize using the phrase that was never used one time in the bible, "Father, Son, Holy Ghost" and those who baptize using the words that were used every time by the New Testament church, "In the name of Jesus Christ" (Acts 2:38, Acts 8:16, Acts 10:48, Acts 19:5, Acts 4:12, Colossians 3:17).

God started his church through his disciples and "added to the church daily such as should be saved" (Acts 2:47). Many churches, which people have assumed to be Christian, are harlot churches. When searching for the true church several questions must be answered and must line up with the Word of God: Acts 2:1-4 and Acts 2:37-47.

1. How do they baptize? Acts 2:38
2. Did they receive the Holy Ghost with the evidence of speaking in other tongues? Acts 2:4
3. Are they continuing in the Apostles' doctrine? Acts 2:42

EXAMINE THE FINDINGS

"There is none other name under heaven given among men, whereby we must be saved" (Acts 4:12).

"Search the scriptures; for in them [you] think [you] have eternal life: and they are they which testify of me, [Jesus]" (John 5:39).

There are many references on the subject of "Jesus name" baptism. The proof that the early disciples baptized using the formula "in the name of Jesus" is as close to you as your public library or home bookshelf. Here is a list of some of them.

1. Britannica Encyclopedia 11ᵗʰ edition Vol. 3, page 365
2. Canney Encyclopedia of Religion, page 53
3. Hastings Encyclopedia of Religion, Vol. 2, page 377, 389
4. Catholic Encyclopedia Vol. 2, page 263
5. Schaff Herzog Religious Encyclopedia Vol. 1, page 435
6. Hastings Dictionary of the Bible, page 88

CHAPTER 10

How to Start a Missionary Department

P roverbs 3:5-6 says, "Trust in the Lord with all thy heart and lean not to thy own understanding. In all thy ways acknowledge him, and he shall direct thy paths."

The first thing to do before beginning any task is to seek the Lord for wisdom and direction. When the time is right, share your burden with the pastor. If this is something that the Lord desires to come forth, he will no doubt have already spoken it into the pastor's heart.

"Wisdom is the principal thing; therefore get wisdom: and in all thy getting get understanding" (Proverbs 4:7). Upon receiving the pastor's blessings, become acquainted with the mission work. Talk to established missionary leaders, visit the library, attend missionary seminars or lecture groups, etc. Learn all you can about this great commission.

Make it known by way of church announcement, word of mouth, flyer, etc. that you seek individuals that have a burning desire to become a part of the missionary department. When there is a response, set a time, date, and place for a meeting. In this first meeting, appoint a temporary president and secretary until officers can be chosen. Keep a record of the meeting.

OFFICERS AND THEIR DUTIES THE PRESIDENT

- Plans, evaluates, and supervises every part of the department
- Must be committed first to God, then to man
- Must be steadfast, unmovable, always abounding in the work of the Lord
- Must be a good listener
- Must be able to hear from God
- Strengthens, encourages, and supports the church, to include tithes and offerings
- Trains individuals to respond to various situations relating to soul winning
- Must have drive and is an industrious person

THE VICE-PRESIDENT

The vice president is second in line to the president, and he performs the same duties as the president upon his/her absence. He may also be responsible for taking charge of a specific area within the missionary department.

THE SECRETARY

- Must maintain an organized and accessible record of minutes
- Is in charge of all letters and correspondence pertaining to this department
- Keeps a listing of all members to include phone numbers and addresses
- Insures that the president has a typed copy of minutes from the previous meeting

THE ASSISTANT SECRETARY

- Performs the same duties as the secretary upon his/her absence

THE TREASURER

- Is responsible for all monies received
- Keeps receipts and an accurate record of all monies disbursed
- Makes records accessible to pastor and president at all times

VARIOUS COMMITTEES AND THEIR DUTIES

PROGRAM COMMITTEE

- Plans programs that are missionary-oriented
- Performs dramas and skits for special occasions (Mother's/Father's Day, Easter)

OUTREACH COMMITTEE

This committee is composed of persons who have a deep concern for lost souls. They seek to call, fellowship with, or visit new members, backsliders, and the sick and shut-in. Their mission takes them into hospitals, nursing homes, and to community doors, compelling souls to be saved.

BAPTISMAL COMMITTEE

This committee is responsible for the care of persons desiring to be baptized in Jesus's name. They insure that towels and robes are ready for all baptisms. After the candidate has repented of his or her sins and is dressed in a robe, the missionary will read Acts 2:38 and Romans 6:1-4. After baptism and redressing, the candidate is to be counseled concerning this new, life-changing experience.

EDUCATION COMMITTEE

Missionaries from this committee teach and train youths, new converts, and others how to be better Christians and how to live holy lives. At times, they are called upon to give short speeches and to appear on programs and other functions.

RECREATION COMMITTEE MOTTO: EDUCATION THROUGH RECREATION

This committee seeks ways to make learning fun. It reaches out to our youth and young adults through such events as vacation Bible school, youth seminars, rapture and day camps, harvest fests, and holiday parties. Some things that can be offered as morale boosters are:

- Appreciation party – appreciate team members for their support and prayers
- Friends and family day – adopt a teen or a new member for the day
- Staff brunch – president appreciates staff for a job well done
- Tributes or certificates – to honor notable service

BYLAWS:

A bylaw is a set of rules that have been adopted by the group for the government of its members and the regulation of its affairs. Each missionary should have in his possession a set of missionary bylaws.

A sample bylaw could include:

- Qualifications of a missionary
- Functions of committee
- Purpose, motto, pledge
- Dues, if applicable
- Dress code, if applicable

GUIDELINE FOR THE ORGANIZATION OF A SMALL MISSIONARY GROUP

JESUS CHRIST

PASTOR

MISSIONARY PRESIDENT

VICE PRESIDENT   SECRETARY

TREASURER

MISSIONARY MEMBERS

GUIDELINE FOR THE ORGANIZATION
OF A LARGE MISSIONARY GROUP

JESUS CHRIST

PASTOR

MISSIONARY PRESIDENT

VICE PRESIDENT   SECRETARY

TREASURER

BAPTISMAL COMMITTEE   OUTREACH COMMITTEE

PROGRAM COMMITTEE   EDUCATION COMMITTEE

MISSIONARY MEMBERS

SAMPLE BYLAWS

MISSIONARY TASK FORCE BYLAWS

According to *Webster's Collegiate Dictionary* a task force is "a temporary grouping under one leader for the purpose of accomplishing a definite objective." "A force is a body of persons or things available for a particular end." A task force can be described as "an individual or group having the power of effective action."

PURPOSE: To win souls for Jesus Christ.

MOTTO: "With Willing, Working Hands, We Will Do God's Will."

PLEDGE: I will continue to be a mountain of light and strength to this church. I will make straight paths for my feet because I am an example to the saints of God. They can look at me and see what they ought to be. I am for the salvation of this church (Acts 13:47).

In the church, a missionary task force consists of ministers, evangelists, and missionaries that work the altar, the upper room, and the baptismal area under the direction of the pastor and missionary president.

QUALIFICATIONS
- Must be in line with the Word of God
- Be a tithe payer
- Willing to obey leadership
- Able to follow instructions
- Faithful to God and the ministry
- Have a desire to learn

FUNCTIONS

A missionary may go to foreign lands to encourage, strengthen, and confirm the will of God. Missionaries of today have demanding positions at their home church. A few of the missionary task force functions are:

- Teaching and training individuals how to respond to various situations relating to soul winning and how to discipline ourselves for the work assigned to us
- Binding up and healing with consolation those who have been wounded by the Word of God
- Strengthening, encouraging, and supporting the church, to include tithing
- Helping to establish baby saints in the church
- Being studied up, prayed up, and fasted up
- Assisting the baptismal committee where needed
- Taking an interest in our young adults
- Working around the altar under the direction of the pastor and the missionary president
- Being alert at all times to assist whenever needed

JUNIOR MISSIONARY
- Greeting visiting children before and after services
- Assisting children to seats after the altar call
- Sitting with children that were baptized while they wait for counseling
- Remaining polite at all times/smiling

THE OUTREACH DEPARTMENT
- Visiting the sick, shut-in, and the elderly
- Lifting up the weak and the backsliders through prayer
- Keeping in contact with visitors, baptismal candidates, and newcomers

- Assisting the doorknockers committee in passing out flyers and church invitations
- Preparing to give short exhortations when called upon for special programs

DRESS CODE: The missionary department may or may not have a dress code.

MEETINGS: Regular department meetings are necessary and informative.

The missionary journey is likened to the work of a medic on the battle field. A missionary's job is to go bravely into the war zone with the mentality of saving lives. Medics wear arm bands to make a statement. The arm band informs the wounded that help is on the way. As missionaries, we are read by the things that we do and say. We are a mountain of light and strength to the church. Medics equip themselves with the tools of their trade such as bandages, stretchers, thermometers, stethoscopes, etc. Likewise, missionaries should equip themselves with bowels of mercy, kindness, humility, meekness, long-suffering, forbearance, forgiveness, and love out of a pure heart (Colossians 3:12-16).

A stasis report is performed, in the field, to determine the condition of a wounded person. Jude verses twenty-two and twenty-three says that we should make a difference between the weak and the willful saint. The weak saint may be saved with tenderness. All one may have to do is airlift him or her to safety through fasting, prayer, and praise. The willful saint will take more effort but can be won over through love and perseverance.

SAMPLE

BYLAWS OF BAPTISMAL COMMITTEE

The purpose of these bylaws is to establish standards that will, by faith, be pleasing in the sight of our Lord and savior, Jesus Christ. The baptismal committee is a group of saints that have been selected by the pastor to perform the duties described in these bylaws. They are grounded in God's word, full of wisdom, and faithful to the house of God. The leader of the committee will be a minister from the pulpit, and he will be the one to perform the baptisms.

THE PROCESS:

Once a candidate has consented to baptism, a member of the baptismal committee will take the candidate into the dressing room. In the dressing room, the primary person will proceed to inform the candadite of the baptism procedure that is to take place. The primary person will read Romans 6:1-4 and Acts 2:38-39. Afterwards, the candidate will be given space to repent and pray.

Word of advice: While in the dressing room, the committee member's job is only to assist the candidate in getting dressed. If the person does not need your help, then leave them alone. The Word has already drawn them, and there is nothing you can say to increase their desire to be saved. The only thing you can possibly be successful in doing is changing their minds, and God may lay their blood on your hands if that person never gets saved.

During this time, the remainder of the committee should be at their proper places, maintaining order and concentrating on the seriousness of what is about to take place.Maintaining order means keeping children, relatives, and anyone else who is not on the committee out of the immediate area. It also means stopping all conversation not pertaining to the baptism. Give a short talk to the candidate and tell him or her what you are about to do.

Baptism is a symbol of repentence. It says to relatives, friends, and to the world that you are turning away from the worldy system and turning to a life with God.

A good spiritual song of praise always helps keep the mind on God. Baptism is serious business, and God will hold you, the committee, directly responsible on how it's performed. A member of the committee will escort the candidate from the dressing room to the baptismal pool. Once helped into the pool, the minister will perform the baptism according to the guidelines given by the pastor. An example is the following: "Willie James Singleton Sr., upon the profession of your faith, in the death, burial, and resurrection of our Lord and Savior Jesus Christ, I now baptize you in the name of Jesus Christ for the remission of your sins, and ye shall receive the gift of the Holy Ghost."After the candidate rises out of the water, the church should be praising God for his goodness.

After the candidate has redressed and receives counseling, jot down his name and phone number and encourage him to come back to the next service. Remember that the team's job isn't finished until everything has been put back in its proper place and the area has been cleaned.

CHAPTER 11

A Missionary Prayer

Have mercy upon me, O God, according to thy loving kindness: according unto the multitude of thy tender mercies blot out my transgressions. Wash me thoroughly from mine iniquities. Keep back thy servant also from secret faults and presumptuous sins; let them not have dominion over me. Let the words of my mouth, and the meditation of my heart, be acceptable in thy sight, O Lord, my strength and my redeemer.

Lead me in the paths of righteousness for thy name's sake. Grant unto thy servant holy boldness to speak thy truth. Uphold me with thy free spirit, open my lips, and my mouth shall show forth thy praises. Then will I teach transgressors thy ways; and sinners shall be converted unto thee.

Give us this day our daily bread and forgive us our debts, as we forgive our debtors, and lead us not into temptation, but deliver us from evil; for thine is the kingdom, and the power, and the glory, forever.

DAILY PRAYER COVER

In the name of Jesus Christ, the anointed one, and by his shed blood and the Word according to St. Matthew 16:19, I bind, rebuke, and bring to naught all divisions and disunity. Through the blood of

Jesus Christ, I put down all rebellion, disobedience, confusion, and disorder. All strife, anger, and wrath must flee. All negative criticism, condemnation, and vain glory, envying, and jealousy must cease. By the power of the Holy Ghost invested in me, I bring into captivity all lying signs and wonders and all evil speech and gossip. I renounce all backbiting, murmuring, complaining, and disputing.

In the Lord only do I put my trust. And no weapon formed against me shall prosper. I am submitted to God, and I wear his whole armor. Therefore, when I resist the devil, he has to flee from me. I take authority over this day in Jesus' name. I declare that Satan is under my feet and will remain there throughout this entire day. In the name of Jesus Christ, I cast Satan out of my life, my family, my mind, my body, my home, my finances, and everything that concerns me.

Lord, I pray for the ministry that you have appointed me to, and I call in ministries of help to assist in this great work. I pray for financial support so that the work will not be hindered. I pray that everyone you send to serve with me will have the same spirit and vision that you have given me and that we will be united in the same understanding, opinions, and judgments. May we stand steadfast in your love and with willing, working hands be forever ready to do your will.

O Lord, we trust in you to direct our footsteps in the straight and narrow way. Teach us to follow after righteousness, godliness, faith, love, patience, meekness, and longsuffering. Help us not to become weary in well doing. Help us to treat others as we desire to be treated. To you be all power, glory, and honor, now and forever. Amen.

CHAPTER 12

Finally My Brethren

All scripture references in this section will come from The
Amplified Bible.

In conclusion, be strong in the Lord (be empowered through
your union with him); draw your strength from Him (that strength
which His boundless might provides). Put on God's whole armor
(the armor of a heavy-armed soldier which God supplies), that you
may be able successfully to stand up against (all) the strategies and
the deceits of the devil. For we are not wrestling with flesh and
blood (contending only with physical opponents), but against the
despotisms, against the powers, against (the master spirits who are)
the world rulers of this present darkness, against the spirit forces of
wickedness in the heavenly (supernatural) sphere.

Therefore put on God's complete armor, that you may be able to
resist and stand your ground on the evil day (of danger), and, having
done all (the crisis demands), to stand (firmly in your place). Stand
therefore (hold your ground), having tightened the belt of truth
around your loins and having put on the breastplate of integrity and
of moral rectitude and right standing with God, and having shod
your feet in preparation (to face the enemy with the firm-footed
stability, the promptness, and the readiness produced by the good
news) of the Gospel of peace.

Lift up over all the (covering) shield of saving faith, upon which you can quench all the flaming missiles of the wicked (one). And take the helmet of salvation and the sword that the Spirit wields, which is the Word of God. Pray at all times (on every occasion, in every season) in the Spirit, with all (manner of) prayer and entreaty. To that end keep alert and watch with strong purpose and perseverance, interceding in behalf of all the saints (God's consecrated people).

And (pray) also for me, that (freedom) of utterance may be given me, that I may open my mouth to proclaim boldly the mystery of the good news (the gospel) (Ephesians 6:10-19).

BIBLIOGRAPHY

Merriam-Webster's Collegiate Dictionary

New American Webster Dictionary

Singleton, Barbara. "Leadership verses Lordship." Christian Education Library. 1999.

Singleton, Barbara D. "Preparation for Fighting Satan." Christian Education Library. 1999.

Singleton, Barbara D. "Rendering the Devil Helpless." Christian Education Library. 1999.

Thomas, Mack Jr. "Baptism and New Birth." Christian Education Library. 1999.

Thomas, Mack Jr. "Restoring a Fallen Soul." Christian Education Library. 2000.

Henson, Robert E. *Effective Altar Ministry.* page 28, 34.

Britannica Encyclopedia 11th edition. Vol. 3. page 365.

Canney Encyclopedia of Religion. page 53.

Hastings Encyclopedia of Religion. Vol. 2. page 377, 389.

Catholic Encyclopedia. Vol. 2. page 263.

Schaff Herzog Religious Encyclopedia. Vol. 1. page 435.

Hastings Dictionary of the Bible. page 88.

The Amplified Bible, Expanded Edition. page 1380.

Printed in the United States
By Bookmasters